SARAH HATTON KNITS

VINTAGE

INSPIRED PROJECTS

SARAH HATTON

First published in Great Britain in 2011 by
Daco Technology Ltd.
www.dacotechnology.co.uk

Designs: Sarah Hatton
Photography: Darren Brant
Styling: Sarah Hatton
Hair & Make-Up: Catherine O'Reilly
Models: Charlotte Reynolds, Freddie Patmore, Karen Rogers
Graphic Design: Darren Brant - CreativeGoo - www.creativegoo.co.uk
Illustration: Teagan White - www.teaganwhite.com
Pattern Checking: Jen Arnall-Culliford
www.sarahhatton.com

ISBN 978-0-9567851-1-4

Introduction

This collection features 7 garments and 2 accessories all with a feminine, vintage feel. I hope you enjoy knitting them as much as I did designing them.

Sarah

Edith Shawl pg. 22

Botany Cardigan pg. 24

Greta Cape/Cardigan pg. 29

Kelly Shrug pg. 31

Lily Shrug pg. 33

Aphrodite Shrug pg. 35

Vivian Scarf pg. 38

Flutterby Cardigan pg. 40

Cosmos Shrug pg. 44

Edith Shawl

YARN
Rowan Kidsilk Haze (shown in Trance 582)
2 x 25gm

YARN AMOUNTS ARE BASED ON AVERAGE
REQUIREMENT AND ARE THEREFORE
APPROXIMATE

FINISHED SIZE
160cm (63¾ in) x 15cm (6in) narrowest and
30cm (11¾ in) widest

NEEDLES
1 pair 4.5mm (UK7/US7) needles

TENSION
17 sts and 33 rows to 10cm over garter stitch
on 4.5mm needles before blocking.

MAIN PART
Cast on 229 sts loosely.
Knit 2 rows.
Next row (RS): *K2tog, yfwd, rep from * to
last st, k1.
Knit 3 rows.

Start shaping
Next row: K127, wrap next st (to wrap st - slip
next st from left hand needle onto right hand
needle, taking yarn to opposite side of work
between the needles and then slipping the
same stitch back onto left hand needle)
and turn,
Next row: K25, wrap next st and turn,
Next row: K29, wrap next st and turn,
Next row: K33, wrap next st and turn,
Next row: K37, wrap next st and turn,
Next row: K41, wrap next st and turn,
Next row: K45, wrap next st and turn,
Next row: K49, wrap next st and turn,
Next row: (K2tog, yfwd) 26 times, k1, wrap
next st and turn,
Next row: K57, wrap next st and turn,
Next row: K61, wrap next st and turn,
Next row: K65, wrap next st and turn,
Next row: K69, wrap next st and turn,
Next row: K73, wrap next st and turn,
Next row: (K2tog, yfwd) 38 times, k1, wrap
next st and turn,
Next row: K81, wrap next st and turn,
Next row: K85, wrap next st and turn,
Next row: K89, wrap next st and turn,
Next row: K95, wrap next st and turn,
Next row: K100, wrap next st and turn,
Next row: (K2tog, yfwd) 52 times, k1, wrap
next st and turn,
Cont to work in garter stitch only working
5 more sts on each row between each wrap st
until the following row has been completed-
Next row: K220, wrap next st and turn, K to
end.

EDGING
Next row: Cast on 17 sts, knit 16 of these sts
then k2tog last st with 1 st from main part of
shawl.
Row 1 (WS): K4, (yfwd, k2tog) 5 times, cast
on 4 sts, k2tog, k1. 20 edging sts.
Row 2: K19, k2tog last st with next st from
main part of shawl.
Row 3: K14, (p1, k1) into next 4 sts, k2.
24 edging sts.
Row 4: K23, k2tog last st with next st from

main part of shawl.
Row 5: K4, (yfwd, k2tog) 5 times, k10.
Row 6: As row 4.
Row 7: Knit to end.
Row 8: Cast off 7 sts, k15, k2tog last st with
next st from main part of shawl.
17 edging sts.
These 8 rows set edging.
Cont as set until all but 1 st of the main part
have been used, then cast off rem sts.

MAKING UP
Soak the shawl in cold water. Remove and roll
in a towel to remove most of the water. Pin
out shawl to the size given and leave until dry.

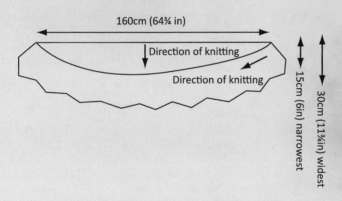

Botany Cardigan

SIZES

S	M	L	XL	XXL	
81-86	91-97	102-107	112-117	122-127	cm
32-34	36-38	40-42	44-46	48-50	in

Actual

89	99	109	119	129	cm
35	39	43	47	51	in

Length

50	54	56	58	60	cm
19¾	21¼	22	22¾	23¾	in

Sleeve

23	24	25	25	26	cm
9	9½	10	10	10¼	in

YARN

Rowan Cashsoft 4 ply (shown in Toxic 459)

7	8	9	10	12	x 50gm

YARN AMOUNTS ARE BASED ON AVERAGE REQUIREMENT AND ARE THEREFORE APPROXIMATE

NEEDLES

1 pair 2.75mm (UK12/US2) needles
1 pair 3.25mm (UK10/US3) needles
1 2.75mm (UK12/US2) circular needle (maybe needed for yoke)
1 3.25mm (UK10/US3) circular needle (maybe needed for yoke)

EXTRAS

3 buttons

TENSION

28 sts and 36 rows to 10cm over st st on 3.25mm needles.

BACK

Using 2.75mm needles, using the thumb method, cast on 133 [147:161:175:189] sts.
** Knit 3 rows.
Row 4 (WS): * P2tog, yrn, rep from * to last st, p1.
Knit 3 rows.
Row 8: P1, * p2tog, yrn, rep from * to last 2 sts, p2.
Rep rows 1 to 7 once.
Next row (WS): Knit. **
Change to 3.25mm needles.
Beg with a K row and working in st st throughout, cont until work meas 10 [11:11:12:12]cm, ending with RS facing for next row.
Next row: K2, ssk, K to last 4 sts, k2tog, k2.
This row sets side seam shaping.
Dec as set on 3 foll 12th rows.
125 [139:153:167:181] sts.
Cont without shaping until work meas 34 [36:37:38:38]cm, ending with RS facing for next row.
Shape raglan
Cast off 4 [5:6:7:8] sts at beg of next 2 rows.
117 [129:141:153:165] sts.
Next row: K2, ssk, K to last 4 sts, k2tog, k2.
Next row: P2, p2tog, P to last 4 sts, p2togtbl, p2.
These 2 rows set raglan shaping.
Dec as set at each end of next 1 [3:7:9:9] foll rows, then on every foll alt row until 95

[99:103:109:115] sts rem.
Work 1 row, ending with RS facing for next row.
Leave rem sts on a holder.

LEFT FRONT

Using 2.75mm needles cast on 74 [82:88:96:102] sts.
Knit 3 rows.
Row 4 (WS): K2, (p2, k1) 3 times, *yrn, p2tog, rep from * to last st, p1.
Row 5: K to last 11 sts, p1, k2tog, yrn, p1, yfwd, ssk, p1, k2tog, yrn, p1, k1.
Row 6: K2, (p2, k1) 3 times, K to end.
Row 7: K to last 11 sts, p1, yfwd, ssk, p1, k2tog, yrn, p1, yfwd, ssk, p1, k1.
Row 8: K2, (p2, k1) 3 times, * p2tog, yrn, rep from * to last st, p1.
Row 9: As row 5.
Row 10: As row 6.
Row 11: As row 7.
Row 12: As row 8.
Row 13: As row 5.
Row 14: As row 6.
Row 15: As row 7.
Row 16: As row 6.
Change to 3.25mm needles.
Row 1: Knit to last 11 sts, p1, k2tog, yrn, p1, yfwd, ssk, p1, k2tog, yrn, p1, k1.
Row 2: K2, (p2, k1) 3 times, P to end.
Row 3: Knit to last 11 sts, p1, yfwd, ssk, p1, k2tog, yrn, p1, yfwd, ssk, p1, k1.
Row 4: K2, (p2, k1) 3 times, P to end.
These 4 rows set patt placement at front edge.
Working in patt throughout cont until work meas 10 [11:11:12:12]cm, ending with RS facing for next row.
Next row: K2, ssk, patt to end.
This row sets side seam shaping.
Dec as set on 3 foll 12th rows.
70 [78:84:92:98] sts.
Cont without shaping until work meas 34 [36:37:38:38]cm, ending with RS facing for next row.

Shape raglan

Next row: Cast off 4 [5:6:7:8] sts, patt to end.
66 [73:78:85:90] sts.
Work 1 row.
Working raglan dec as set on back, dec 1 st at raglan edge of next 3 [5:6:8:10] rows.
63 [68:72:77:80] sts.
Work 1 [1:0:0:0] row straight.
Shape front neck
At the same time as working the short row shaping given below, dec 1 st at raglan side of next 1 [1:3:3:1] rows and on foll 7 [9:10:11:14] alt rows:-
Next 2 rows: Working decrease, K to last 13 [15:13:13:18] sts, wrap next st (by slipping next st from left needle to right, taking yarn to opposite side of work between needles and then slipping same st back onto left hand needle) and turn (leaving all remaining sts unworked), P to end, working decrease if needed for your size.
Next 2 rows: K to last 18 [19:17:17:21] sts, wrap next st and turn, P to end.
Next 2 rows: K to last 23 [23:21:21:24] sts, wrap next st and turn, P to end.
Next 2 rows: K to last 28 [27:25:25:27] sts, wrap next st and turn, P to end.
Continuing to work decreases as set, work 4 [6:8:9:11] more pairs of short rows with 5 [4:4:4:3] more sts left unworked on each set – final pair of short rows will start, K to last 48 [51:57:61:60] sts.
Leave rem sts on a holder.

RIGHT FRONT

Using 2.75mm needles cast on 74 [82:88:96:102] sts.
 Knit 3 rows.
Row 4 (WS): P1, * p2tog, yrn, rep from * to last 11 sts, (k1, p2) 3 times, k2.
Row 5: K1, p1, k2tog, yrn, p1, yfwd, ssk, p1, k2tog, yrn, p1, K to end.
Row 6: K to last 11 sts, (k1, p2) 3 times, k2.
Row 7: K1, p1, yfwd, ssk, p1, k2tog, yrn, p1, yfwd, ssk, p1, K to end.
Row 8: P1, * yrn, p2tog, rep from * to last 11 sts, (k1, p2) 3 times, k2.

Row 9: As row 5.
Row 10: As row 6.
Row 11: As row 7.
Row 12: As row 8.
Row 13: As row 5.
Row 14: As row 6.
Row 15: As row 7.
Row 16: As row 6.
Change to 3.25mm needles.
Row 1: K1, p1, k2tog, yrn, p1, yfwd, ssk, p1, k2tog, yrn, p1, K to end.
Row 2: P to last 11 sts, (k1, p2) 3 times, k2.
Row 3: K1, p1, yfwd, ssk, p1, k2tog, yrn, p1, yfwd, ssk, p1, K to end.
Row 4: P to last 11 sts, (k1, p2) 3 times, k2.
These 4 rows set patt placement for front edge.
Working in patt throughout cont until work meas 10 [11:11:12:12]cm, ending with RS facing for next row.
Next row: Patt to last 4 sts, k2tog, k2.
This row sets side seam shaping.
Dec as set on 3 foll 12th rows.
70 [78:84:92:98] sts.
Cont without shaping until work meas 34 [36:37:38:38]cm, ending with WS facing for next row.
Shape raglan
Next row: Cast off 4 [5:6:7:8] sts, patt to end.
66 [73:78:85:90] sts.
Working raglan dec as set on back, dec 1 st at raglan edge of next 3 [5:5:7:9] rows.
63 [68:73:78:81] sts.
Shape front neck
At the same time as working the short row shaping given below, dec 1 st at raglan side of next 0 [0:4:4:2] rows and on foll 8 [10:10:11:14] alt rows:-
Next 2 rows: Working decrease if needed for your size, P to last 13 [15:13:13:18] sts, wrap next st (by slipping next st from left needle to right, taking yarn to opposite side of work between needles and then slipping same st back onto left hand needle) and turn (leaving all remaining sts unworked), K to end, working decrease.
Next 2 rows: P to last 18 [19:17:17:21] sts,

wrap next st and turn, K to end.
Next 2 rows: P to last 23 [23:21:21:24] sts, wrap next st and turn, K to end.
Next 2 rows: P to last 28 [27:25:25:27] sts, wrap next st and turn, K to end.
Continuing to work decreases as set, work 4 [6:8:9:11] more pairs of short rows with 5 [4:4:4:3] more sts left unworked on each set – final pair of short rows will start, P to last 48 [51:57:61:60] sts.
Patt 1 WS row across all sts, when working wrapped sts, purl the wrapped st and the wrapping loop tog as one stitch.
Leave rem sts on a holder.

SLEEVES (Make 2 alike)
Using 2.75mm needles cast on 73 [75:79:85:91] sts.
Work from ** to ** as set on back.
Change to 3.25mm needles and cont as folls:-
Row 1: K30 [31:33:36:39], work next 12 sts at set on row 1 of chart, K to end.
Row 2: P30 [31:33:36:39], work next 12 sts as set on row 2 of chart, P to end.
Row 3: K2, m1 (by picking up loop between last and next st and working into the back of this loop), k28 [29:31:34:37], work next 12 sts as set on row 3 of chart, K to last 2 sts, m1, k2. 75 [77:81:87:93] sts.
Row 4: P31 [32:34:37:40], work next 12 sts as set on row 4 of chart, P to end.
Row 5: (K2, m1) 0 [0:0:1:1] times, k31 [32:34:35:38], work next 11 sts at set on row 5 of chart, K to last 0 [0:0:2:2] sts, m1, k2. 75 [77:81:89:95] sts.
Row 6: P31 [32:34:38:41], work next 12 sts as set on row 6 of chart, P to end.
Row 7: K2, m1, k29 [30:32:36:39], work next 12 sts as set on row 7 of chart, K to last 2 sts, m1, k2. 77 [79:83:91:97] sts.
Row 8 and every foll alt row: Purl.
Row 9: (K2, m1) 0 [0:0:1:1] times, k32 [33:35:37:40], work next 12 sts as set on row 9 of chart, K to last 0 [0:0:2:2] sts, (m1, k2) 0 [0:0:1:1] times. 77 [79:83:93:99] sts.
Row 11: (K2, m1) 0 [1:1:0:0] times, k32 [31:33:40:43], work next 12 sts as set on row

11 of chart, K to last 0 [2:2:0:0] sts, (m1, k2) 0 [1:1:0:0] times. 77 [81:85:93:99] sts.

Row 13: (K2, m1) 1 [0:0:1:1] times, k30 [34:36:38:41], work next 12 sts as set on row 13 of chart, K to last 2 [0:0:2:2] sts, (m1, k2) 1 [0:0:1:1] times. 79 [81:85:95:101] sts.

Beg with a P row and working in st st throughout, inc 1 st at set at each end of 6th [2nd:2nd:4th:4th] row then on every foll 6th [4th:4th:4th:4th] row to 95 [105:111:123:135] sts, then on 0 [1:1:0:0] foll 0 [6th:6th:0:0] row. 95 [107:113:123:135] sts.

Cont without shaping until sleeve meas 23 [24:25:25:26]cm, ending with RS facing for next row.

Shape raglan

Cast off 4 [5:6:7:8] sts at beg of next 2 rows. 87 [97:101:109:119] sts.

Working dec as set on back, dec 1 st at each end of next and 8 [8:2:2:2] foll rows, then on every alt row to 59 [63:69:73:77] sts.

Work 1 row, ending with RS facing for next row.

Leave rem sts on a holder.

YOKE

With RS facing, using 2.75mm circular needle, patt across 55 [58:59:63:65] sts from right front, K59 [63:69:73:77] sts from holder for sleeve, K95 [99:103:109:115] sts from back, K59 [63:69:73:77] sts from sleeve and patt across 55 [58:59:63:65] sts from left front (when working wrapped sts, knit the wrapped st and the wrapping loop tog as one stitch). 323 [341:359:381:399] sts.

Row 1 (WS): Patt 11 sts, K to last 11 sts, patt 11 sts.

Row 2: Patt 11 sts, k13 [10:7:22:7], * k2tog, k6 [6:6:6:8], rep from * to last 27 [24:21:36:21] sts, k2tog, k14 [11:8:23:8], patt 11 sts. 288 [303:318:341:362] sts.

Row 3: As row 1.

Change to 3.25mm needles.

Row 4: Patt 11 sts, K to last 11 sts, patt 11 sts.

Row 5: Patt 11 sts, * p2tog, yrn, rep from * to last 11 [12:11:12:11] sts, p0 [1:0:1:0], patt 11 sts.

Row 6: As row 4.

Row 7: As row 1.

Row 8: Patt 11 sts, K2tog, k11[8:5:20:5] * K2tog, k5[5:5:5:7], rep from * to last 26 [23:20:35:20] sts, k2tog, k11[8:5:20:5], k2tog, patt 11 sts. 251[263:276:299:323] sts.

Row 9: As row 1.

Row 10: Patt 11 sts, working 12 st rep from chart row 1 19 [20:21:23:25] times, K1, patt 11 sts.

This row sets chart placement.

Work all 13 rows from chart, keeping 1 sts st st at end of left front, and 11 sts at front edges in patt.

Row 23: As row 1.

Row 24: Patt 11 sts, K13 [10:7:22:7], * k2tog, k4 [4:4:4:6], rep from * to last 25 [22:19:34:19] sts, k2tog, k12 [9:6:21:6], patt 11 sts. 218 [227:236:261:288] sts.

Row 25: As row 1.

Row 26: As row 4.

Row 27: Patt 11 sts, * p2tog, yrn, rep from * to last 11 [12:11:12:11] sts, p0 [1:0:1:0], patt 11 sts.

Row 28: As row 4.

Row 29: As row 1.

Row 30: Patt 11 sts, k13 [10:7:22:7], * k2tog, k3 [3:3:3:5], rep from * to last 24 [21:18:33:18] sts, k2tog, k11 [8:5:20:5], patt 11 sts. 183 [189:195:221:251] sts.

Row 31: Patt 11 sts, p1, * p2tog, yrn, rep from * to last 11 sts, patt 11 sts.

Row 32: As row 4.

Row 33: As row 1.

Row 34: Patt 11 sts, k13 [10:7:22:7], * k2tog, k2 [2:2:2:4], rep from * to last 23 [20:17:32:17] sts, k2tog, k10 [7:4:19:4], patt 11 sts. 148 [151:154:181:214] sts.

Row 35: Patt 11 sts, * p2tog, yrn, rep from * to last 11 [12:11:12:11] sts, p0 [1:0:1:0], patt 11 sts.

Row 36: Patt 11 sts, K to last 11 sts, patt 11 sts.

Change to 2.75mm needles and knit 2 rows. Cast off knitways on WS.

MAKING UP

Press as described on ball band.

Join side and sleeve seams. Join raglan seams. Sew three buttons equally spaced in to right front yoke section as shown.

SLEEVE & YOKE CHART

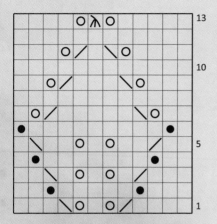

23[24:25:25:26]cm
9[9½:10:10:10¼]in

50[54:56:58:60]cm
19¾[21¼:22:22¾:23¾]in

44.5[49.5:54.5:59.5:64.5]cm
17½[19½:21½:23½:25½:]in

	RS: knit stitch WS: purl stitch
/	RS: Knit two stitches together as one stitch
O	RS: Yarn Over
\	RS: Slip one stitch as if to knit, Slip another stitch as if to knit. Insert left-hand needle into front of these 2 stitches and knit them together
●	RS: purl stitch WS: knit stitch
⋏	RS: slip 1, k2tog, pass slip stitch over k2tog

28

Greta Cape/ Cardigan

SIZES

S	M	L	
81-91	97-107	112-122	cm
32-36	38-42	44-48	in

Finished length (after blocking)

29	37	44	cm
11½	14½	17½	in

YARN
Rowan Cashsoft 4 ply (shown in Quartz 446)

3	4	5	x 50gm

YARN AMOUNTS ARE BASED ON AVERAGE
REQUIREMENT AND ARE THEREFORE
APPROXIMATE

NEEDLES
1 pair 2.75mm (UK12/US2) needles
1 pair 3.25mm (UK10/US3) needles
1 pair 4mm (UK8/US6) needles

TENSION
28 sts and 36 rows to 10cm over st st on
3.25mm needles.

Using 4mm needles cast on 291 [331:371] sts
loosely or using the lace method.
Knit 2 rows.
Cont as folls:-
Row 1: K3, * (k2tog) 3 times, k1, (yfwd, k1)
6 times, (k2tog) 3 times, rep from * to last 3
sts, k3.
Row 2: K3, purl to last 3 sts, k3.
Row 3: Knit.
Row 4: Knit.
Rows 5 to 7: As rows 1 to 3.
Row 8: As row 2.
Row 9: Knit.
Row 10: Knit.
These 10 rows set patt.
Work 14 [34:54] rows more in patt, ending
with RS facing for next row.
Change to 3.25mm needles and work 6 rows
more in patt.
Row 31/51/71: K3, * (k2tog) 3 times, k2,
(yfwd, k1) 4 times, k1, (k2tog) 6 times, k1,
(yfwd, k1) 6 times, (k2tog) 3 times, rep from *
to last 22 sts, (k2tog) 3 times, k2, (yfwd, k1) 4
times, k1, (k2tog) 3 times, k3.
275 [311:347] sts.
Work 3 rows in patt.
Row 35/55/75: K3, * (k2tog) 3 times, (yfwd,
k1) 5 times, yfwd, (k2tog) 6 times, k2, (yfwd,
k1) 4 times, k1, (k2tog) 3 times, rep from * to
last 20 sts, (k2tog) 3 times, (yfwd, k1) 5 times,
yfwd, (k2tog) 3 times, k3. 261 [295:329] sts.
Work 5 rows in patt.
Row 41/61/81: K3, * (k2tog) 3 times, k1,
(yfwd, k1) 4 times, (k2tog) 6 times, (yfwd, k1)
5 times, yfwd, (k2tog) 3 times, rep from * to
last 20 sts, (k2tog) 3 times, k1, (yfwd, k1) 4
times, (k2tog) 3 times, k3. 245 [277:309] sts.
Work 3 rows in patt.
Row 45/65/85: K3, * (k2tog) twice, k2, (yfwd,
k1) 4 times, k1, (k2tog) 5 times, k1, (yfwd, k1)
4 times, (k2tog) 3 times, rep from * to last 18
sts, (k2tog) twice, k2, (yfwd, k1) 4 times, k1,
(k2tog) twice, k3. 231 [261:291] sts.

Work 5 rows in patt.

Row 51/71/91: K3, * (k2tog) 3 times, (yfwd, k1) 3 times, yfwd, (k2tog) 5 times, k2, (yfwd, k1) 4 times, k1, (k2tog) twice, rep from * to last 18 sts, (k2tog) 3 times, (yfwd, k1) 3 times, yfwd, (k2tog) 3 times, k3. 215 [243:271] sts.
Work 3 rows in patt.

Row 55/75/95: K3, * (k2tog) twice, k1, (yfwd, k1) 4 times, (k2tog) 5 times, (yfwd, k1) 3 times, yfwd, (k2tog) 3 times, rep from * to last 16 sts, (k2tog) twice, k1, (yfwd, k1) 4 times, (k2tog) twice, k3. 201 [227:253] sts.
Work 5 rows in patt.

Row 61/81/101: K3, * (k2tog) twice, k2, (yfwd, k1) twice, k1, (k2tog) 4 times, k1, (yfwd, k1) 4 times, (k2tog) twice, rep from * to last 16 sts, (k2tog) twice, k2, (yfwd, k1) twice, k1, (k2tog) twice, k3. 185 [209:233] sts.
Work 3 rows in patt.

Row 65/85/105: K3, * (k2tog) twice, yfwd, (k1, yfwd) 3 times, (k2tog) 4 times, k2, (yfwd, k1) twice, k1, (k2tog) twice, rep from * to last 14 sts, (k2tog) twice, yfwd, (k1, yfwd) 3 times, (k2tog) twice, k3. 171 [193:215] sts.
Work 5 rows in patt.

Row 71/91/111: K3, * (k2tog) twice, (k1, yfwd) twice, k1, (k2tog) 4 times, yfwd, (k1, yfwd) 3 times, (k2tog) twice, rep from * to last 14 sts, (k2tog) twice, (k1, yfwd) twice, k1, (k2tog) twice, k3. 155 [175:195] sts.
Work 3 rows in patt.

Row 85/101/121: K3, * k2tog, k2, (yfwd, k1) twice, k1, (k2tog) 3 times, (k1, yfwd) twice, k1, (k2tog) twice, rep from * to last 12 sts, k2tog, k2, (yfwd, k1) twice, k1, k2tog, k3. 141 [159:177] sts.
Work 2 rows, ending with WS facing for next row.
Change to 2.75mm needles.
Knit 1 row.

Next row (RS): K0 [4:0], * k4, k2tog, k4 [4:5], rep from * to last 1 [5:1] sts, k1 [5:1]. 127 [144:161] sts.
Knit 1 row.

Next row (buttonhole row): K2, k2tog, yfwd, k6, k2tog, yfwd, knit to end.
Knit 2 rows.
Cast off knitways on WS.

MAKING UP
Sew in ends. Wet block as you would a shawl. Sew on buttons – 2 to neckband to match buttonholes and two on inside lower edge of back at underarm to be used to turn your cape into a shrug cardigan.

Kelly Shrug

SIZES

S	M	L	XL	XXL	
81-86	91-97	102-107	112-117	122-127	cm
32-34	36-38	40-42	44-46	48-50	in

Actual

104	114	124	134	143	cm
41	45	48¾	52¾	56½	in

Length

49	51	53	55	57	cm
19½	20	21	21½	22½	in

Sleeve

45	46	46	46	47	cm
17½	18	18	18	18¼	in

YARN

Rowan Kid Classic (shown in Tattoo 856)

6	7	8	9	9	x50gm

YARN AMOUNTS ARE BASED ON AVERAGE
REQUIREMENT AND ARE THEREFORE
APPROXIMATE

NEEDLES

1 pair 4.5mm (UK7/US7) needles
1 pair 5mm (UK6/US8) needles

TENSION

19 sts and 25 rows to 10cm over st st on 5mm
needles.

EXTRAS

2 buttons (optional)

BODY (worked in one piece from cuff to cuff)

Using 4.5mm needles and thumb method
cast on 45 [49:51:53:53] sts.
Row 1 (RS): K2 [1:2:3:3], * yfwd, ssk, p1,
k2tog, yfrn, p1, rep from * to last 7 [6:7:8:8]
sts, yfwd, ssk, p1, k2tog, yfwd, k2 [1:2:3:3].
Row 2: P4 [3:4:5:5], * k1, p2, rep from * to
last 2 [1:2:3:3] sts, p2 [1:2:3:3].
Row 3: K2 [1:2:3:3], * k2tog, yfrn, p1, yfwd,
ssk, p1, rep from * to last 7 [6:7:8:8] sts,
k2tog, yfwd, p1, yfwd, ssk, k2 [1:2:3:3].
Row 4: As row 2.
These 4 rows set ric rac patt.
Work a further 8 rows in patt, ending with RS
facing for next row.
Change to 5mm needles.
Next row: K2, m1, K to last 2 sts, m1, k2.
This row sets sleeve shaping.
Working in stocking stitch, inc as set at each
end of 3 [9:13:7:18] foll 6th [6th:6th:4th:4th]
rows, then on 9 [5:2:11:4] foll 8th
[8th:8th:6th:6th] rows. 71 [79:83:91:99] sts.
Work 9 rows without shaping, ending with RS
facing for next row. (Sleeve should now meas
45 [46:46:46:47]cm)
Cast on 5 sts at beg of next 6 rows.
101 [109:113:121:129] sts.
Cast on 43 [42:43:45:44] sts at beg of next 2
rows. 187 [193:199:211:217] sts.
Next row: Knit.
Next row: K3, P to last 3 sts, k3.
These 2 rows set patt.
Work a further 44 [50:56:62:68] rows in patt,
ending with RS facing for next row.
Change to 4.5mm needles and cont as folls:-
Row 1: K3, * p1, k2tog, yfrn, p1, yfwd, ssk,

rep from * to last 4 sts, p1, k3.

Row 2: K4, * p2, k1, rep from * to last 3 sts, k3.

Row 3: K3, * p1, yfwd, ssk, p1, k2tog, yfrn, rep from * to last 4 sts, p1, k3.

Row 4: K4, * p2, k1, rep from * to last 3 sts, k3.

These 4 rows set patt.

Work 8 rows more in patt, ending with RS facing for next row.

Next row: Cast off 93 [96:99:105:108] sts, patt to end. 94 [97:100:106:109] sts.

Next row: Patt to end, cast on 93 [96:99:105:108] sts.

187 [193:199:211:217] sts.

Beg with row 3, work 12 rows more in patt, ending with RS facing for next row.

Change to 5mm needles.

Work a further 44 [50:56:62:68] rows in st st and g st edging, ending with RS facing for next row.

Cast off 43 [42:43:45:44] sts at beg of next 2 rows. 101 [109:113:121:129] sts.

Working in st st only, cast off 5 sts at beg of next 6 rows. 71 [79:83:91:99] sts.

Work 10 rows without shaping, ending with RS facing for next row.

Next row: K2, ssk, K to last 4 sts, k2tog, k2.

This row sets sleeve shaping.

Dec 1 st as set at each end of 9 [5:2:11:4] foll 8th [8th:8th:6th:6th] rows, then on every foll 6th [6th:6th:4th:4th] row to 45 [49:51:53:53] sts.

Work 1 row, ending with RS facing for next row.

Change to 4.5mm needles and work 12 rows in ric rac patt as set on first cuff.

Cast off in patt.

MAKING UP

Press as described on ball band.

Join side and sleeve seams.

Sew on buttons as shown if desired.

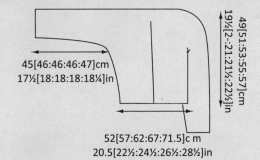

45[46:46:46:47]cm
17½[18:18:18:18¼]in

49[51:53:55:57]cm
19¼[2-:21:21½:22½]in

52[57:62:67:71.5]c m
20.5[22½:24½:26½:28½]in

Lily Shrug

SIZES

S	M	L	XL	XXL	
81-86	91-97	102-107	112-117	122-127	cm
32-34	36-38	40-42	44-46	48-50	in

Width

89	103	114	127	141	cm
35	40½	44½	50	55½	in

Length

37	38	40	42	44	cm
14½	15	15¾	16½	17¼	in

YARN
Rowan Cocoon (shown in Bilberry 812)

3	3	4	5	6	x 100gm

YARN AMOUNTS ARE BASED ON AVERAGE REQUIREMENT AND ARE THEREFORE APPROXIMATE

NEEDLES
1 pair 6mm needles (UK4/US10)
1 5.5mm crochet hook (for corsage)

EXTRAS
2 buttons (1 for corsage)

TENSION
16 sts and 20 rows to 10cm over patt on 6mm needles.

BODY (worked in one piece)
Using 6mm needles cast on 143 [165:183:203:225] sts.
Row 1 (RS): K2, * yfwd, k2togtbl, rep from * to last st, k1.
Row 2: K1, * p1, k1, rep from * to end.
Row 3: K2, * p1, k1, rep from * to last st, k1.
Row 4: As row 2.
Row 5: K1, (k1, p1) 3 times, K to last 7 sts, (p1, k1) 3 times, k1.
Row 6: K1, (p1, k1) 3 times, P to last 7 sts, (k1, p1) 3 times, k1.
These 2 rows set st st and rib edging.
Cont as set until work meas 11 [12:13:14:15] cm, ending with WS facing for next row.
Next row (WS): Patt 30 [35:38:42:46], (k1, p1) 7 [8:9:10:11] times, k1, p53 [61:69:77:87], (k1, p1) 7 [8:9:10:11] times, k1, patt to end.
Next row: Patt 30 [35:38:42:46], cast off 15 [17:19:21:23] sts in rib, p53 [61:69:77:87], cast off 15 [17:19:21:23] sts in rib, patt to end.
Next row: Patt 30 [35:38:42:46], turn and using lace/knitted on method cast on 34 [38:42:46:50] sts, turn, k53 [61:69:77:87], turn and using lace method cast on 34 [38:42:46:50] sts, turn and patt to end. 181 [207:229:253:279] sts.
Next row: Patt 29 [34:37:41:45], k2tog, k1, (yfwd, k2togtbl) 16 [18:20:22:24] times, k52 [60:68:76:86], k2tog, k1, (yfwd, k2togtbl) 16 [18:20:22:24] times, patt to end. 179 [205:227:251:277] sts.
Next row: Patt 30 [35:38:42:46], p1, (k1, p1) 16 [18:20:22:24] times, p53 [61:69:77:87], p1, (k1, p1) 16 [18:20:22:24] times, patt to end.
Shape raglan
Row 1: Patt 26 [31:34:38:42], **k2tog, (yfwd, sl2, k1, p2sso, yfwd - to create decorative lace), ssk,** k27 [31:35:39:43], rep from ** to **, k45 [53:61:69:79], rep from ** to **,

k27 [31:35:39:43], rep from ** to **, patt 26 [31:34:38:42]. 171 [197:219:243:269] sts.
Row 2: Patt 7, P to last 7 sts, patt 7.
These 2 rows set raglan shaping.
Dec 1 st at front and back raglan edge of next and 3 [9:14:14:14] foll alt rows then on 5 [2:0:0:0] foll 4th rows and AT THE SAME TIME dec 1 st at each end of sleeves on next and 6 [9:6:9:14] foll alt rows, then on 3 [2:4:2:0] foll 4th rows.
Work 1 row, ending with RS facing for next row. 95 [101:115:135:149] sts.

Shape front neck
Cont to work shaping as set, dec 1 st at body raglan edge of 3rd [3rd:3rd:1st:1st] and 2 [2:2:6:7] foll alt rows, and on sleeves on 3rd [3rd:3rd:1st:1st] and foll 0 [0:0:0:1] foll alt row, then on 2 [2:2:3:3] foll 4th rows **AND AT SAME TIME** use short row shaping to shape neck as folls:-
Row 1: Patt to last 4 sts, wrap next st (by slipping next st from left needle to right, taking yarn to opposite side of work between needles and then slipping same st back onto left hand needle – when working back across wrapped sts, work the wrapped st and the wrapping loop tog as one stitch) and turn, leaving all remaining sts unworked.
Row 2: Patt to last 4 sts, wrap next st and turn.
Row 3: Patt to last 6 sts, wrap next st and turn.
Row 4: Patt to last 8 sts, wrap next st and turn.
Cont working shaping, work 2 sts more between wrap sts until the following row has been completed:-
Next row (RS): Patt to last 14 [14:14:16:18] sts, wrap next st and patt to end.
71 [77:91:91:97] sts.
Next row: K2, * p1, k1, rep from * to last st, k1.
This row sets rib placement.
Working in rib as set on hem cont as folls:-
Next row: Rib to last 6 sts, p2tog, yon, rib to end.

Work 1 row more in rib.
Next row (WS): K1, p1, * yrn, p2togtbl, rep from * to last st, k1.
Cast off in rib.

CORSAGE
Using 5.5mm hook make 4 ch, ss to join and form loop.
Next round: 1 dc, work 8 dc into loop, ss to join.
Next round: 1 ch, 1 dc, 1 dc into next dc, 2 dc into next dc, rep from * to end of round, ss to join.
Next round: 1ch, 1 dc, * (1 dc into next dc) twice, 2 dc into next dc, rep from * to end of round, ss to join.
Next round: * 9 ch, ss into front only of next dc, rep to end.
Next round: * 13 ch, ss into back only of next dc, rep to end. Fasten off.

44.5[51.5:57:63.5:70.5]cm
17½[20¼:22¼:25:27¾]in

37[38:40:42:44]cm
14½[15:15¾:16½:17¾]in

Aphrodite Shrug

NEEDLES
1 pair 2.75mm (UK12/US2) needles
1 pair 3.25mm (UK10/US3) needles

TENSION
24 sts and 36 rows to 10cm over patt on 3.25mm needles (after blocking and relaxed).

RIGHT SIDE (starting at front neck)
Using 3.25mm needles cast on 65 [71:77:85:95] sts.
Row 1 (RS): Knit.
Row 2: K2, P to last 2 sts, k2.
Row 3: K2 [5:2:6:5], work all stitches from chart repeating centre 12 st rep 4 [4:5:5:6] times, K to end.
Row 4: K2, P to last 2 sts, k2
Last 2 rows set g st and st st at edges and pattern placement.
Cont as set, working 14 row rep 5 [5:5:6:6] times, ending with RS facing for next row.
Now repeating rows 13 and 14 only work 5 [9:13:1:5] rows, ending with WS facing for next row. (This should leave you at the front edge.)
Place marker to denote armhole.
Working in row 13 and 14 patt throughout cont as folls:-

Shape side
****Next row:** Patt 5 [8:5:9:8], wrap next st (by slipping next st from left needle to right, taking yarn to opposite side of work between needles and then slipping same st back onto left hand needle) and turn (on all following rows pick up and work wrap loop together with st), patt to end.
Next row: Patt 11 [14:11:15:14], wrap next st and turn, patt to end.
Next row: Patt 17 [20:17:21:20], wrap next st and turn, patt to end.
Next row: Patt 23 [26:23:27:26], wrap next st and turn, patt to end.
Next row: Patt 29 [32:29:33:32], wrap next st and turn, patt to end.
Next row: Patt 35 [38:35:39:38], wrap next st and turn, patt to end.
Next row: Patt 41 [44:41:45:44], wrap next st and turn, patt to end.
Next row: Patt 47 [50:47:51:50], wrap next st and turn, patt to end.
Next row: Patt 53 [56:53:57:56], wrap next st and turn, patt to end.

SIZES

S	M	L	XL	XXL	
81-86	91-97	102-107	112-117	122-127	cm
32-34	36-38	40-42	44-46	48-50	in

Actual width (before gathering)

54	59	64	71	79	cm
21¼	23¼	25¼	28	31	in

Length

27	28.5	30	31	33	cm
10½	11¼	11¾	12	13	in

Sleeve Length

2	cm
1	in

YARN
Rowan Fine Lace (shown in Vintage 926)

2	2	2	3	3 x 50gm

YARN AMOUNTS ARE BASED ON AVERAGE REQUIREMENT AND ARE THEREFORE APPROXIMATE

Next row: Patt 59 [62:59:63:62], wrap next st and turn, patt to end.
For M, L, XL and XXL only
Next row: Patt [68:65:69:68], wrap next st and turn, patt to end.
For L, XL and XXL only
Next row: Patt [71:75:74], wrap next st and turn, patt to end.
For XL and XXL only
Next row: Patt [81:80], wrap next st and turn, patt to end.
For XXL only
Next row: Patt [86], wrap next st and turn, patt to end.***
Working rows appropriate for each size work from *** to ** so the shaping rows are reversed.
Place marker to denote armhole.
Work 5 [9:13:1:5] rows, ending with RS facing for next row.
Work full chart 14 row rep as set at beg of right side 5 [5:5:6:6] times, ending with RS facing for next row.
Next row: Knit.
Next row: K2, P to last 2 sts, k2.
Leave rem sts on a holder.

LEFT SIDE (starting at front neck)
Using 3.25mm needles cast on 65 [71:77:85:95] sts.
Row 1 (RS): Knit.
Row 2: K2, P to last 2 sts, k2.
Row 3: K2 [5:2:6:5], work from chart repeating centre 12 st rep 4 [4:5:5:6] times, K to end.
Row 4: K2, P to last 2 sts, k2.
Last 2 rows set g st edges and pattern placement.
Cont as set, working 14 row rep 5 [5:5:6:6] times, ending with RS facing for next row.
Now repeating rows 13 and 14 only work 6 [10:14:2:6] rows, ending with RS facing for next row. (This should leave you at the front edge)
Place marker to denote armhole.
Working in patt throughout cont as folls:-
Shape side
**Next row: Patt 5 [8:5:9:8], wrap next st and turn (on all following rows pick up and work wrap loop together with st), patt to end.
Next row: Patt11 [14:11:15:14], wrap next st and turn, patt to end.
Next row: Patt 17 [20:17:21:20], wrap next st and turn, patt to end.

Next row: Patt 23 [26:23:27:26], wrap next st and turn, patt to end.
Next row: Patt 29 [32:29:33:32], wrap next st and turn, patt to end.
Next row: Patt 35 [38:35:39:38], wrap next st and turn, patt to end.
Next row: Patt 41 [44:41:45:44], wrap next st and turn, patt to end.
Next row: Patt 47 [50:47:51:50], wrap next st and turn, patt to end.
Next row: Patt 53 [56:53:57:56], wrap next st and turn, patt to end.
Next row: Patt 59 [62:59:63:62], wrap next st and turn, patt to end.
For M, L, XL and XXL only
Next row: Patt [68:65:69:68], wrap next st and turn, patt to end.
For L, XL and XXL only
Next row: Patt [71:75:74], wrap next st and turn, patt to end.
For XL and XXL only
Next row: Patt [81:80], wrap next st and turn, patt to end.
For XXL only
Next row: Patt [86], wrap next st and turn, patt to end.***
Working rows appropriate for each size work from *** to ** so the shaping rows are reversed.
Place marker to denote armhole.
Work 6 [10:14:2:6] rows, ending with RS facing for next row.
Work 14 row rep as set at beg of right side 5 [5:5:6:6] times, ending with RS facing for next row.
Next row: Knit.
Next row: K2, P to last 2 sts, k2.
Leave rem sts on a holder.

SLEEVES (Make 2 alike)
Using 2.75mm needles cast on 81 [89:97:103:113] sts.
Knit 4 rows.
Change to 3.25mm needles.
Row 1 (RS): K3 [1:5:2:1], * yfwd, sl1, k2tog, psso, yfwd, k3, rep from * to last 0 [4:2:5:4] sts, (yfwd, sl1, k2tog, psso, yfwd) 0 [1:0:1:1] times, k0 [1:2:2:1].
Row 2: Purl.
These 2 rows set patt.
Working in patt thoughout, cont as folls:-
Work 4 rows, ending with RS facing for next row.

Shape raglan
Next row: K1, sl1, k1, psso, patt to last 3 sts, k2tog, k1.
This row sets raglan shaping.
Dec 1 st as set at each end of next 8 [6:4:4:1] foll 4th rows, then on every foll alt row to 21 [21:21:25:25] sts.
Work 1 row, ending with RS facing for next row.
Leave rem sts on a holder.

MAKING UP
Join body sections to sleeve raglans as folls:-
Match first sleeve raglan to front, from cast-on edge down to marker, and sew in place. Then match same sleeve to same body piece from marker to stitches on holder. Sew in place and repeat for second sleeve.
Join both pieces along the row-end edge for approx. 7 [8:9:10:11]cm, from where you have stitches on hold, to create back seam of garment.

NECKBAND CASING
Using 2.75mm needles pick up and knit 65 [71:77:85:95] sts along cast-on edge of right body, K21 [21:21:25:25] sts from sleeve top, K65 [71:77:85:95] sts from stitch holder of right body, K65 [71:77:85:95] sts from holder of left body, K21 [21:21:25:25] sts from sleeve top and pick up and knit 65 [71:77:85:95] sts from cast-on edge of left front.
302 [326:350:390:430] sts.
Next row (WS): K6 [9:3:5:7], * k2tog, k16, rep from * to last 8 [11:5:7:9] sts, k2tog, k6 [9:3:5:7]. 285 [308:330:368:406] sts.
Next row: K6 [9:3:5:7], * k2tog, k15, rep from * to last 7 [10:4:6:8] sts, k2tog, k5 [8:2:4:6]. 268 [290:310:346:382] sts.
Beg with a P row, work 6 rows in st st.
Next row (WS) ridge row: Knit.
Beg with a K row, work 8 rows in st st.
Using 3.25mm needles cast off loosely.
Fold neckband at ridge row and slip stitch in place on WS of garment.

MAKING UP
Press as described on the ball band.
Feed ribbon through casing. You can now try your garment on and move the gathers at the neck edge so that it sits nicely on the body.

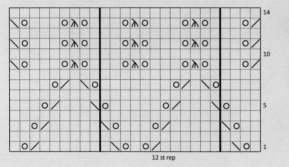

12 st rep

RS: knit stitch
WS: purl stitch

RS: Knit two stitches together as one stitch

O RS: Yarn Over

RS: Slip one stitch as if to knit, Slip another stitch as if to knit. Insert left-hand needle into front of these 2 stitches and knit them together

RS: slip 1, k2tog, pass slip stitch over k2tog

27[28.5:30:31:33]cm
10¾[11¼:11¾:12:13]in

Vivian Shawl

YARN
Rowan Lace (shown in Quaint 925)
1 x 25gm
AND
Rowan Kidsilk Haze (shown in Blushes 583)
2 x 25gm
1 END OF EACH YARN HELD AND WORKED
TOGETHER THROUGHOUT

YARN AMOUNTS ARE BASED ON AVERAGE
REQUIREMENT AND ARE THEREFORE
APPROXIMATE

FINISHED SIZE (relaxed after blocking)
148cm (58½in) x 67cm (26½in)

NEEDLES
1 pair 5.5mm (UK5/US9) needles

TENSION
16 sts and 18 rows to 10cm over patt on
5.5mm needles before blocking. 14 sts and 29
rows to 10cm over st st, relaxed after blocking.

Using 1 end of each yarn at same time
throughout, cast on 7 sts.
Knit 2 rows.

Row 1 (RS): K2, (yfwd, k1) 3 times, yfwd, k2.
11 sts.
Row 2 and every foll alt row: K2, P to last 2
sts, k2.
Row 3: K2, place marker, yfwd, k3, yfwd,
place marker, k1, place marker, yfwd, k3,
yfwd, place marker, k2. 15 sts.
Row 5: K2, slip marker, yfwd, K to marker,
yfwd, slip marker, k1, slip marker, yfwd, K to
marker, yfwd, slip marker, k2. 19 sts.
This row sets shaping and 2 sts in g st at each
end.
The markers show the two sts in g st at each
end of the row, as well as the central st,
which is worked in st st throughout. Cont
shaping as set, increasing 1 st at each end of
the two marked sections, on every RS row
until there are 247 sts (If you wish to make
your shawl larger you will need to ensure you
finish with a multiple of 12 plus 7).
Work 1 row, removing markers.
Next row (RS): K2, yfwd, place marker, work
12 st rep as set on row 1 of chart 10 times,
place marker, (k1, yfwd) twice, k1, place
marker, work 12 st rep as set on row 1 of
chart 10 times, place marker, yfwd, k2.
251 sts.
Next row: K2, P to last 2 sts, k2.
Next row: K2, yfwd, k1, slip marker, work 12
st rep as set on row 3 of chart 10 times, slip
marker, k2, yfwd, k1, yfwd, k2, slip marker,
work 12 st rep as set on row 3 of chart 10
times, slip marker, k1, yfwd, k2. 255 sts.
Using markers as a guide for chart pattern
placement and working increases as set,
cont until all 16 rows of chart have been
completed, ending with RS facing for next
row. 279 sts.
Knit 4 rows.
Cast off row: Cast off 1 st, * slip st back onto
LH needle, (take yarn over the needle, then
pass the st over this loop) 4 times, cast off 2
sts, rep from * to end. Fasten off. These loop
chains will give you a looser edge to help with
blocking, however if you wish to turn them
into a more decorative feature simply work
more yon, psso's to create a longer chain
between stitches.

MAKING UP

Soak the shawl in cold water. Remove and roll in a towel to remove most of the water. Pin out shawl to the size given and leave until dry.

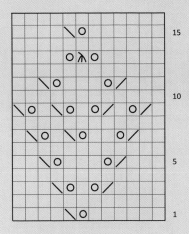

RS: knit stitch
WS: purl stitch

RS: Knit two stitches together as one stitch

RS: Yarn Over

RS: Slip one stitch as if to knit, Slip another stitch as if to knit. Insert left-hand needle into front of these 2 stitches and knit them together

RS: slip 1, k2tog, pass slip stitch over k2tog

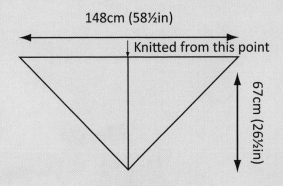

148cm (58½in)

Knitted from this point

67cm (26½in)

YARN AMOUNTS ARE BASED ON AVERAGE
REQUIREMENTS AND ARE THEREFORE
APPROXIMATE

NEEDLES
1 pair 3.25mm (UK10/US3) needles
1 pair 4mm (UK8/US6) needles

EXTRAS
5 buttons

TENSION
23 sts and 30 rows to 10cm over st st on 4mm
needles.

SPECIAL ABBREVIATIONS
MW – (make wings) place needle from front
to back into centre of stitch 3 sts to the left
and 2 rows below, pull yarn through the centre
of this st, leave this st on RH needle and slip
next st to LH needle then knit both these 2 sts
together through the back loops, k3, place LH
needle into the same place as before, pull yarn
through centre of st and place on left hand
needle, then k2togtbl this loop and the next st.

Flutterby Cardigan

SIZES

S	M	L	XL	XXL	
81-86	91-97	102-107	112-117	122-127	cm
32-34	36-38	40-42	44-46	48-50	in

Actual

90	100	110	117	130	cm
35½	39½	43¼	46	51¼	in

Length

52	55	57	59	61	cm
20½	21¾	22½	23¼	24	in

Sleeve

45	46	46	46	47	cm
17½	18	18	18	18½	in

YARN

Rowan Wool Cotton (shown in Gypsy 910)

9	10	11	12	13 x 50gm

BACK

Using 4mm needles, using the thumb method,
cast on 123 [135:151:159:177] sts.
Row 1: K1, * p1, k1, rep from * to end.
This row sets moss stitch.
Cont in moss st until work meas 7 [8:9:
11:12]cm, ending with RS facing for next row.
Next row: Patt 6 [12:8:12:9], * patt3tog,
patt 9, rep from * to last 9 [15:11:15:12],
patt3tog, patt 6 [12:8:12:9].
103 [115:127:135:149] sts.
Change to 3.25mm needles and cont in moss
st for a further 3cm, ending with RS facing for
next row.
Change to 4mm needles.
Row 1 (RS): Knit.
Row 2: Purl.
Rows 3 and 4: As rows 1 and 2.
Row 5: K1 [7:1:5:2], (k2, place needle into
centre of st in same position as 1st of these
sts but 2 rows below, pull yarn through the

centre of this st and place on the LH needle, then k2togtbl this loop and the next st, k7) 0 [0:0:0:1] times, * MW, k7, rep from * to last 6 [12:6:10:17] sts, MW, k1 [7:1:5:7], (place needle into centre of st 3 sts to the left but 2 rows below, pull yarn through the centre of this st and place on the LH needle, then k2togtbl this loop and the next st) 0 [0:0:0:1] times, k0 [0:0:0:4].

Row 6: Purl.

Rows 7 to 10: As rows 1 and 2.

Row 11: K7 [1:7:1:6], (k2, place needle into centre of st in same position as 1st of these sts but 2 rows below, pull yarn through the centre of this st and place on the LH needle, then k2togtbl this loop and the next st, k7) 0 [0:0:1:0] times, * MW, k7, rep from * to last 12 [6:12:4:11] sts, (MW) 1[1:1:0:1] times, (place needle into centre of st 3 sts along but 2 rows below, pull yarn through the centre of this st and place on the LH needle, then k2togtbl this loop and the next st) 0 [0:0:1:0] times, k7 [1:7:3:6].

Row 12: Purl.

These 12 rows set patt.

Cont in patt as set until work meas 31 [33:34:35:36] cm, ending with RS facing for next row.

Shape armholes

Keeping pattern correct throughout, cast off 5 [6:7:7:8] sts at beg of next 2 rows. 93 [103:113:121:133] sts.

Next row: K2, sl1, k1, psso, patt to last 4 sts, k2tog, k2.

Next row: P2, p2tog, patt to last 4 sts, p2togtbl, p2. 89 [99:109:117:129] sts.

These 2 rows set armhole shaping.

Dec 1 st at each end of 3 [3:7:7:9] foll rows, then on 1 [2:1:2:2] foll alt rows. 81 [89:93:99:107] sts.

Cont without shaping until armhole meas 20 [21:22:23:24]cm, ending with RS facing for next row.

Shape shoulders and back neck

Next row: Patt 20 [24:25:28:31], turn and leave rem sts on a holder.

Work each side of neck separately.

Next row (WS): Cast off 3 sts, patt to end. 17 [21:22:25:28] sts.

Next row (RS): Cast off 8 [10:11:12:14] sts, patt to end. 9 [11:11:13:14] sts.

Work 1 row.

Cast off rem sts.

With RS facing, rejoin yarn to rem sts, cast off centre 41 [41:43:43:45] sts, patt to end. Complete to match first side of neck, reversing all shapings.

LEFT FRONT

Using 4mm needles, using the thumb method, cast on 59 [65:73:77:87] sts.

Row 1: K1, * p1, k1, rep from * to end. This row sets moss stitch.

Cont in moss st until work meas 7 [8:9:11:12]cm, ending with RS facing for next row.

Next row: Patt 6 [12:8:12:9], * patt3tog, patt 9, rep from * to last 5 [5:5:5:6] sts, patt3tog, patt 2 [2:2:2:3]. 49 [55:61:65:73] sts.

Change to 3.25mm needles.

Next row: Cast on 8 sts, patt across these and rem sts. 57 [63:69:73:81] sts.

Work in moss st for a further 3cm, ending with **WS** facing for next row.

Next row (WS): Patt 8 and leave these 8 sts on a holder, patt to end, dec 0 [0:0:0:1] st at end of row. 49 [55:61:65:72] sts.

Change to 4mm needles.

Row 1 (RS): Knit.

Row 2: Purl.

Rows 3 and 4: As rows 1 and 2.

Row 5: K1 [7:1:5:2], (k2, place needle into centre of st in same position as 1st of these sts but 2 rows below, pull yarn through the centre of this st and place on the LH needle, then k2togtbl this loop and the next st, k7) 0 [0:0:0:1] times, * MW, k7, rep from * end.

Row 6: Purl.

Rows 7 to 10: As rows 1 and 2.

Row 11: K7 [1:7:1:6], (k2, place needle into centre of st in same position as 1st of these sts but 2 rows below, pull yarn through the centre of this st and place on the LH needle, then k2togtbl this loop and the next st, k7)

0 [0:0:1:0] times, * MW, k7, rep from * to last 6 sts, MW, k1.

Row 12: Purl.

These 12 rows set patt.

Cont in patt until work matches back to start of armhole shaping, ending with RS facing for next row.

Shape armhole

Next row: Cast off 5 [6:7:7:8] sts, patt to end. 44 [49:54:58:64] sts.

Work 1 row.

Next row: K2, sl1, k1, psso, patt to end.

Next row: Patt to last 4 sts, p2togtbl, p2. 42 [47:52:56:62] sts.

These 2 rows set armhole shaping.

Dec 1 st at armhole edge of 3 [3:7:7:9] foll rows, then on 1 [2:1:2:2] foll alt rows. 38 [42:44:47:51] sts.

Cont without shaping until armhole meas 7 [8:8:9:9]cm, ending with **WS** facing for next row.

Shape front neck

Next row: Cast off 8 sts, patt to end. 30 [34:36:39:43] sts.

Dec 1 st at neck edge of next 5 rows, then on 6 [6:6:6:7] foll alt row, then on every foll 4th row to 17 [21:22:25:28] sts.

Cont without shaping until armhole matches back to start of shoulder shaping, ending with RS facing for next row.

Shape shoulder

Next row (RS): Cast off 8 [10:11:12:14] sts, patt to end. 9 [11:11:13:14] sts.

Work 1 row.

Cast off rem sts.

RIGHT FRONT

Using 4mm needles, using the thumb method, cast on 59 [65:73:77:87] sts.

Row 1: K1, * p1, k1, rep from * to end.

This row sets moss stitch.

Cont in moss st until work meas 7 [8:9:11:12] cm, ending with RS facing for next row.

Next row: Patt 2 [2:2:2:3], patt3tog, * patt 9, patt3tog, rep from * to last 6 [12:8:12:9] sts, patt 6 [12:8:12:9]. 49 [55:61:65:73] sts.

Change to 3.25mm needles.

Work 1 row.

Next row: Cast on 8 sts, patt across these and rem sts. 57 [63:69:73:81] sts.

Work in moss st for a further 1cm, ending with RS facing for next row.

Next row: Patt 3, cast off 2 sts (to form buttonhole), patt to end.

Next row: Patt to end, cast on 2 sts over gap created by casting off on previous row.

Complete until moss st matches left front, ending with RS facing for next row.

Next row (WS): Patt 8 and leave these 8 sts on a holder, patt to end, dec 0 [0:0:0:1] st at end of row. 49 [55:61:65:72] sts.

Work 1 row.

Change to 4mm needles.

Row 1 (RS): Knit.

Row 2: Purl.

Rows 3 and 4: As rows 1 and 2.

Row 5: K7, * MW, k7, rep from * to last 6 [12:6:10:17] sts, MW, k1 [7:1:5:7], (place needle into centre of st 3 sts to the left but 2 rows below, pull yarn through the centre of this st and place on the LH needle, then k2togtbl this loop and the next st) 0 [0:0:0:1] times, k0 [0:0:0:4].

Row 6: Purl.

Rows 7 to 10: As rows 1 and 2.

Row 11: K1, * MW, k7, rep from * to last 12 [6:12:4:11] sts, (MW) 1[1:1:0:1] times, (place needle into centre of st 3 sts along but 2 rows below, pull yarn through the centre of this st and place on the LH needle, then k2togtbl this loop and the next st) 0 [0:0:1:0] times, k7 [1:7:3 6].

Row 12: Purl.

These 12 rows set patt.

Complete to match left front, reversing all shapings.

SLEEVES

Using 3.25mm needles cast on 55[59:63:65:65] sts.

Working in moss st as set on back work 8 rows.

Change to 4mm needles.

Working in moss st, inc 1 st at each end of 3rd

and foll 8th [8th:8th:6th:6th] row.
59 [63:67:69:69] sts.
Work 3 [3:3:5:5] rows more.
Cont as folls:-

Row 1 (RS): (Inc in 1st st) 0 [0:0:1:1] times, K to last 0 [0:0:2:2] sts, (inc in next st, k1) 0 [0:0:1:1] times. 59 [63:67:71:71] sts.

Row 2: Purl.

Row 3: Knit.

Row 4: Purl.

Row 5: (Inc in 1st st) 1 [1:1:0:0] times, k2 [4:6:9:9], * MW, k7, rep from * to last 8 [10:12:14:14] sts, MW, k1 [3:5:9:9], (inc in next st, k1) 1 [1:1:0:0] times. 61 [65:69:71:71] sts.

Row 6: Purl.

Rows 7 to 10: As rows 1 to 4. 61 [65:69:73:73] sts.

Row 11: K4 [6:8:10:10] * MW, k7, rep from * to last 9 [11:13:15:15] sts, MW, k4 [6:8:10:10].

Row 12: Purl.

These 12 rows set patt and start shaping. Working inc sts into patt, working half patterns as on 5th and 6th sizes of back if desired, inc 1 st at each end of next and 6 [4:9:5:14] foll 8th [8th:8th:6th:6th] rows then on every foll 10th [10th:10th:8th:8th] row to 83 [87:93:101:105] sts.
Cont without shaping until sleeve meas 45 [46:46:46:47]cm, ending with RS facing for next row.

Shape sleeve top
Cast off 5 [6:7:7:8] sts at beg of next 2 rows. 73 [75:79:87:89] sts.
Dec 1 st at each end of next 5 [5:5:11:11] rows, then on every foll alt row to 41 sts, dec 1 st at each end of next 3 rows. 35 sts.
Cast off 5 sts at beg of next 4 rows. 15 sts.
Cast off rem 15 sts.

MAKING UP
Join shoulder seams.

BUTTON BAND
Rejoin yarn to sts left on a holder on left front and using 3.25mm needles cont in moss st

as set until band fits up front edge to start of neck shaping, sewing in position as same time and ending with RS facing for next row, return sts to a holder.
Place markers for buttons on left front, the first to fall in same place as first buttonhole made on right front and the last will fall 1cm into the neckband so place 3 markers evenly between these 2 points.

BUTTONHOLE BAND
Rejoin yarn to sts left on a holder for right front, using 3.25mm needles cont in moss st as set, working buttonholes as set to match markers on buttonband, sewing in position at same time until band fits up front edge to start of neck shaping, ending with RS facing for next row.
DO NOT BREAK OFF YARN.
NECKBAND
Patt across 8 sts of buttonhole band, pick up and knit 45 [45:49:49:51] sts up right side of neck, 49 [49:51:51:53] sts from back neck, 45 [45:49:49:51] sts down left side of neck and 8 sts from buttonband.
155 [155:165:165:171] sts.
Working in moss st as set by back, work 3 rows.

Next row (RS): Patt 3, cast off 2 sts, patt to end.

Next row: Patt to last 3 sts, cast on 2 sts over gap created by casting off sts on previous row.
Work 4 rows.
Cast off in patt.

Press as described on ball band.
Join side and sleeve seams. Sew sleeves into position using the set in method and easing to fit. Sew on buttons.

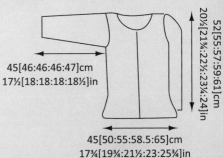

45[46:46:46:47]cm
17½[18:18:18:18½]in

52[55:57:59:61]cm
20½[21¾:22½:23¾:24]in

45[50:55:58.5:65]cm
17¾[19¾:21½:23:25¾]in

Cosmos Shrug

NEEDLES
1 pair 2.75mm (UK12/US2) needles
1 pair 3.25mm (UK10/US3) needles

EXTRAS
Approximately 100 [100:100:120:120] size 8/0 beads
Sewing needle and cotton for threading beads
1 small button

TENSION
30 sts and 32 rows to 10cm over st st on 3.25mm needles.

SPECIAL ABBREVIATIONS AND NOTES

Before starting your knitting you will need to thread beads onto your yarn. Thread a fine sewing needle with sewing thread. Knot the ends of the sewing thread together to create a loop before passing the end of your yarn through this loop. Thread a bead onto the needle and pull gently down onto yarn.

Pb - place bead by bringing yarn to front of work, slide bead up yarn so that it sits close to work, slip next st and take yarn to back of work, leaving a bead sitting in front of slipped stitch.

SIZES

S	M	L	XL	XXL	
81-86	91-97	102-107	112-117	122-127	cm
32-34	36-38	40-42	44-46	48-50	in

Actual

93	103	114	125	136	cm
36¾	40½	45	49½	53½	in

Length

37	39	41	42	46	cm
14½	15½	16	16½	18	in

Sleeve

2	2	2	2	2	cm
1	1	1	1	1	in

YARN

Rowan Kidsilk Haze (shown in Majestic 589)

3	3	4	4	5x25gm	

YARN AMOUNTS ARE BASED ON AVERAGE REQUIREMENT AND ARE THEREFORE APPROXIMATE

BACK

Using 2.75mm needles, cast on 139 [153:169:187:203] sts.
Row 1 (RS): K1, * p1, k1, rep from * to end.
Row 2: * P1, k1, rep from * to last st, p1.
These 2 rows set rib.
Work 4 rows more in rib.
Change to 3.25mm needles.
Beg with a K row and working in st st throughout cont until work meas 18 [19:20:20:22]cm, ending with RS facing for next row.

Shape armholes
Cast off 5 [6:7:8:10] sts at beg of next 2 rows.
129 [141:155:171:183] sts.
Next row: K2, ssk, K to last 4 sts, k2tog, k2.
Next row: P2, p2tog, P to last 4 sts, p2togtbl, p2. 125 [137:151:167:179] sts.
These 2 rows set shaping.
Dec 1 st as set at each end of next 3 [5:7:11:11]

rows, then on 5 [6:7:6:6] foll alt rows.
109 [115:123:133:145] sts.
Cont without shaping until armhole meas 17
[18:19:20:22]cm, ending with RS facing for
next row.

Shape back neck
Next row: K32 [35:36:41:45] sts and turn,
leaving rem sts on a holder .
Work each side of neck separately.
Cast off 3 sts at beg of next and foll alt row.
26 [29:30:35:39] sts.

Shape shoulder
Cast off 13 [14:15:17:19] sts at beg of next
row. 13 [15:15:18:20] sts.
Work 1 row.
Cast off rem sts.
With RS facing, working on rem sts, cast off
centre 45 [45:51:51:55] sts, K to end.
Complete to match first side of neck,
reversing all shapings.

LEFT FRONT
Thread approximately a third of the beads
onto your yarn.
Using 2.75mm needles cast on
70 [78:86:94:102] sts.
Row 1 (RS): * K1, p1, rep from * to last 2 sts,
k2.
Row 2: * K1, p1, rep from * to end.
Row 3: * K1, p1, rep from * to last 4 sts, pb,
p1, k2.
Row 4: As row 2.
Rows 5 and 6: As rows 1 and 2.
Change to 3.25mm needles.
Row 1: K to last 5 sts, p1, pb, p1, k2.
Row 2: K1, (p1, k1) twice, P to end.
Row 3: K to last 5 sts, p1, k1, p1, k2.
Row 4: As row 2.
These 4 rows set patt.
Cont in patt as set until front matches back
to start of armhole shaping, ending with RS
facing for next row.

Shape armhole
Next row: Cast off 5 [6:7:8:10] sts, patt to
end. 65 [72:79:86:92] sts.
Work 1 row.
Working dec as set on back, dec 1 st at

armhole edge of next 5 [7:9:13:13] rows, then
on 5 [6:7:6:6] foll alt rows.
55 [59:63:67:73] sts.
Cont without shaping until armhole meas
7 [8:8:9:11]cm, ending with **WS** facing for
next row.
Next row: Cast off 9 [10:10:10:10] sts, P to
end. 46 [49:53:57:63] sts.
Dec 1 st at neck edge of next
13 [13:13:13:15] rows, then on every foll alt
row to 26 [29:30:35:39] sts.
Cont without shaping until left front matches
back to start of shoulder shaping, ending with
RS facing for next row.

Shape shoulder
Cast off 13 [14:15:17:19] sts at beg of next
row. 13 [15:15:18:20] sts.
Work 1 row.
Cast off rem sts.

RIGHT FRONT
Thread approximately a third of the beads
onto your yarn.
Using 2.75mm needles cast on
70 [78:86:94:102] sts.
Row 1 (RS): K2, * p1, k1, rep from * to end.
Row 2: * P1, k1, rep from * to end.
Row 3: K2, p1, pb, * p1, k1, rep from * to end.
Row 4: As row 2.
Rows 5 and 6: As rows 1 and 2.
Change to 3.25mm needles.
Row 1: K2, p1, pb, p1, K to end.
Row 2: P to last 5 sts, k1, (p1, k1) twice.
Row 3: K to last 5 sts, p1, k1, p1, k2.
Row 4: As row 2.
These 4 rows set patt.
Complete as given for left front, reversing all
shapings.

SLEEVES (Make 2 alike)
Using 2.75mm needles cast on
103 [107:111:115:125] sts.
Work 6 rows in rib as given for back.
Change to 3.25mm needles, beg with a K row
and work in st st throughout, cont as folls:-
Work 2 rows.

Shape sleeve top
Cast off 5 [6:7:8:10] sts at beg of next 2 rows.
93 [95:97:99:105] sts.
Dec 1 st at each end of next 5 rows, then on
every foll alt row until 65 sts rem, then on 13
foll rows, ending with RS facing for next row.
39 sts.
Cast off 5 sts at beg of next 4 rows. 19 sts.
Cast off rem sts.

Join both shoulder seams.

NECK TRIM
Thread remaining beads onto yarn.
Using 3.25mm needles cast on
149 [149:164:164:179] sts.
Row 1 (RS): K2, *pb, k2, rep from * to end.
Row 2: Knit to end, **and AT SAME TIME** dec 2
[2:1:1:0] sts evenly across row.
147 [147:163:163:179] sts.
Row 3: K2, * yfwd, k6, s11, k2tog, psso, k6,
yfwd, k1, rep from * to last st, k1.
Row 4 and every foll alt row: K2, P to last 2
sts, k2.
Row 5: K2, * k1, yfwd, k5, sl1, k2tog, psso, k5,
yfwd, k2, rep from * to last st, k1.
Row 7: K2, * k2, yfwd, k4, sl1, k2tog, psso, k4,
yfwd, k3, rep from * to last st, k1.
Row 9: K2, * k3, yfwd, k3, sl1, k2tog, psso,
k3, yfwd, k4, rep from * to last st, k1.
Row 11: K2, * k4, yfwd, k2, sl1, k2tog, psso,
k2, yfwd, k5, rep from * to last st, k1.
Row 13: K2, * k5, yfwd, k1, sl1, k2tog, psso,
k1, yfwd, k6, rep from * to last st, k1.
Row 15: K2, * k6, yfwd, sl1, k2tog, psso, yfwd,
k7, rep from * to last st, k1.
Row 16: As row 4.
Work rows 3 to 7 once more, ending with **WS**
facing for next row.
Next row: P26 [26:34:34:24], p2tog, (p1,
p2tog) 31 [31:31:31:43] times, P to end.
115 [115:131:131:135] sts.
Leave sts on a spare needle.

NECKBAND
With RS facing, using 2.75mm needles, pick
up and knit 43 [43:47:47:47] sts up right neck,
57 [57:63:63:67] sts from back neck and 43
[43:47:47:47] sts down left side of neck.
143 [143:157:157:161] sts.
Knit 1 row.
Next row (RS): K14 [14:13:13:13], holding sts
of trim in front of main body and working 1
st from trim together with st from neckband
cont until all sts from trim have been worked
and joined to neckband, k14 [14:13:13:13].
Knit 3 rows.
Next row: K2, * p1, k1, rep from * to last st,
k1.
Next row: * K1, p1, rep from * to last st, k1.
These 2 rows set rib.
Next row: Rib 3, rib2tog, (yrn) twice, rib2tog,
rib to end.
Work 4 rows more in rib, working into front
and back of double yrn to form a buttonhole.
Cast off in rib.

MAKING UP
Press as described on ball band.
Join side and sleeve seams. Sew in sleeves
using the set in method. Sew on button.

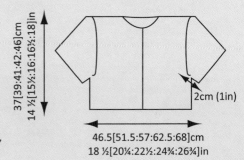

37[39:41:42:46]cm
14 ½[15½:16:16½:18]in

2cm (1in)

46.5[51.5:57:62.5:68]cm
18 ½[20¼:22½:24¾:26¾]in

Useful information and abbreviations

TENSION

Knitting to the correct tension is vital to all knitted garments as it will affect the finished size and shape. Before starting your project we would recommend that you knit a tension square to check that you are able to achieve the tension that the pattern has been written to. If you have too many stitches to 10cm we recommend trying a larger needle, if you have to few stitches to 10cm we recommend using a smaller needle. If the correct tension has been achieved the size of your garment should be the same as the size diagram given at the end of the pattern.

SIZING NOTES

Once you have checked your tension the next step is to choose which size to knit. The table at the front of the pattern gives the width all the way round the body (with the exception of Aphrodite) whilst those on the size diagram at the end of the pattern are ½ of the body width so that you can use it as a reference whilst knitting your project.

FINISHING INSTRUCTIONS

We would recommend pressing all garments as given on the ball band and using the size diagram as a guide to the size. Pressing instructions for scarves/shawls are given in the pattern.
If the ball band suggested that the yarn should not be pressed we recommend that you pin the garment out to size and cover with damp cloths and leave until dry.
When sewing up your garment we recommend using mattress stitch unless otherwise stated.

Beads from:
www.debbieabrahamsbeads.co.uk

CHART NOTES

When working from charts all RS rows are read from right to left and WS from left to right.

ABBREVIATIONS

K – knit
P – purl
St(s) – stitches
Inc – increase
Dec – decrease
St st – stocking stitch (1 row K, 1 row P)
Beg – beginning
Foll – following
Rem – remaining
Cont – continue
Tog – together
Cm – centimetres
Mm – millimetres
In(s) – inch(es)
RS – right side
WS – wrong side
Psso – pass slipped stitch over
Yfwd – yarn forward
Meas – measures
Rep – repeat
Ssk – slip the next two stitches separately before placing left hand needle through both stitches and knitting them together
Sl1 – slip one stitch
Yrn – yarn round needle
Tbl – through back of loop
M1 – make one stitch (by picking up loop between last and next st and working into the back of this loop)
Yfrn – yarn forward and around needle
patt - pattern
p2sso - pass 2 slipped stitch over
LH - left hand
RH - right hand
Yrn - yarn round needle

CROCHET ABBREVIATIONS

Ch – chain
Ss – slip stitch
Dc – double crochet/US – single crochet

Stockist List

AUSTRALIA: Australian Country Spinners, Pty Ltd, Level 7, 409 St. Kilda Road, Melbourne Vic 3004.
Tel: 03 9380 3830 Email: sales@auspinners.com.au

AUSTRIA: Coats Harlander GmbH, Autokaderstrasse 31, A -1210 Wien. Tel: (01) 27716 – 0

BELGIUM: Coats Benelux, Ring Oost 14A, Ninove, 9400, Belgium Tel: 0346 35 37 00
Email: sales.coatsninove@coats.com

CANADA: Westminster Fibers Inc, 165 Ledge St, Nashua, NH03060 Tel: (1 603) 886 5041 / 5043
Email: rowan@westminsterfibers.com

CHINA: Coats Shanghai Ltd, No 9 Building , Baosheng Road, Songjiang Industrial Zone, Shanghai.
Tel: (86- 21) 5774 3733 Email: victor.li@coats.com

DENMARK: Coats Danmark A/S, Nannasgade 28, 2200 Kobenhavn N Tel: (45) 35 86 90 50
Fax: (45) 35 82 15 10 Email: info@hpgruppen.dk
Web: www.hpgruppen.dk

FINLAND: Coats Opti Oy, Ketjutie 3, 04220 Kerava
Tel: (358) 9 274 871

FRANCE: Coats France / Steiner Frères, SAS 100, avenue du Général de Gaulle, 18 500 Mehun-Sur-Yèvre
Tel: (33) 02 48 23 12 30 Web: www.coatscrafts.fr

GERMANY: Coats GmbH, Kaiserstrasse 1, D-79341 Kenzingen Tel: (49) 7644 8020 Web: www.coatsgmbh.de

HOLLAND: Coats Benelux, Ring Oost 14A, Ninove, 9400, Belgium Tel: 0346 35 37 00
Email: sales.coatsninove@coats.com

HONG KONG: Coats China Holdings Ltd, 19/F Millennium City 2, 378 Kwun Tong Road, Kwun Tong, Kowloon
Tel: (852) 2798 6886 Fax: (852) 2305 0311

ICELAND: Storkurinn, Laugavegi 59, 101 Reykjavik
Tel: (354) 551 8258 Email: storkurinn@simnet.is

ITALY: Coats Cucirini s.r.l., Via Sarca 223, 20126 Milano
Tel: 800 992377 Email: servizio.clienti@coats.com

KOREA: Coats Korea Co Ltd, 5F Kuckdong B/D, 935-40 Bangbae-Dong, Seocho-Gu, Seoul Tel: (82) 2 521 6262.
Fax: (82) 2 521 5181

LEBANON: y.knot, Saifi Village, Mkhalissiya Street 162, Beirut Tel: (961) 1 992211 Email: y.knot@cyberia.net.lb

LUXEMBOURG: Coats Benelux, Ring Oost 14A, Ninove, 9400,Belgium Tel: 054 318989
Email: sales.coatsninove@coats.com

MALTA: John Gregory Ltd, 8 Ta'Xbiex Sea Front, Msida MSD 1512, Malta
Tel: +356 2133 0202, Email: raygreg@onvol.net

MEXICO: Estambres Crochet SA de CV, Aaron Saenz 1891-7, Monterrey, NL 64650 Mexico
Tel: +52 (81) 8335-3870

NEW ZEALAND: ACS New Zealand, 1 March Place, Belfast, Christchurch. Tel: 64-3-323-6665

NORWAY: Coats Knappehuset AS, Pb 100 Ulset, 5873 Bergen. Tel: (47) 55 53 93 00

SINGAPORE: Golden Dragon Store, 101 Upper Cross Street #02-51, People's Park Centre, Singapore 058357.
Tel: (65) 6 5358454 Email: gdscraft@hotmail.com

SOUTH AFRICA: Arthur Bales LTD, 62 4th Avenue, Linden 2195 Tel: (27) 11 888 2401 Email: arthurb@new.co.za

SPAIN; Coats Fabra, Santa Adria 20, 08030 Barcelona Tel: 932908400
Email: atencion.clientes@coats.com

SWEDEN: Coats Expotex AB, Division Craft, JA Wetterg-rensgatta 7, Vastra Frolunda, 431 30 Goteburg Goteborg
Tel: (46) 33 720 79 00

SWITZERLAND: Coats Stroppel AG, CH -5300 Turgi (AG)
Tel: (41) 562981220

TAIWAN: Cactus Quality Co Ltd, 7FL-2, No 140, Roosevelt Road, Sec 2,Taipei, Taiwan, R.O.C.
Tel: 886-2-23656527 Email: cqcl@m17.hinet.net

THAILAND: Global Wide Trading, 10 Lad Prao Soi 88, Bangkok 10310. Tel: 00 662 933 9019
Email: global.wide@yahoo.com

U.S.A.: Westminster Fibers Inc, 8 Shelter Drive, Greer South Carolina, NH03060.
Tel: 800 445-9276
Email: rowan@westminsterfibers.com

U.K: Rowan, Green Lane Mill, Holmfirth, West Yorkshire, England HD9 2DX.
Tel: +44 (0) 1484 681881 Fax: +44 (0) 1484 687920
Email: mail@knitrowan.com
Web: www.knitrowan.com

For stockists in all other countries please contact Rowan for details